FIRST REPERTOIRE F
DESCANT RECORDER

with piano

edited and selected by
ausgewählt und herausgegeben von
choisi et édité par

Sally Adams

FABER *ff* MUSIC

© 2004 by Faber Music Ltd
First published in 2004 by Faber Music Ltd
Bloomsbury House 74–77 Great Russell Street London WC1B 3DA
Cover illustration by Drew Hillier
Music processed by Donald Sheppard
Printed in England by Caligraving Ltd

ISBN10: 0-571-52328-5
EAN13: 978-0-571-52328-3

To buy Faber Music publications or to find out about the full range of titles available
please contact your local music retailer or Faber Music sales enquiries:

Faber Music Limited, Burnt Mill, Elizabeth Way, Harlow, CM20 2HX England
Tel: +44 (0)1279 82 89 82   Fax: +44 (0)1279 82 89 83
sales@fabermusic.com   fabermusic.com

CONTENTS

Off to somewhere

Sarah Watts

Les bouffons

from *Orchésographie* (1589)

Traditional,
arr. Bergmann

Pony trot

Walter Bergmann

Austrian ländler

Walter Bergmann

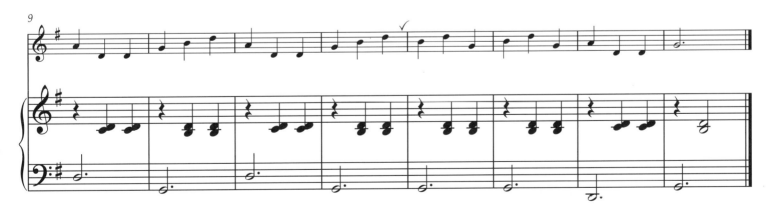

Waltzing echidna

An echidna is an Australian animal with spikes, somewhat like a hedgehog.

Elissa Milne

Theme

from *Theme and variations for flute and strings*

Saverio Mercadante
(1795–1870)
arr. Adams

Monty
(The mystery cat)

Pam Wedgwood

Musette

Esprit Philippe Chèdeville
(1696–1762)
arr. Bergmann

Minuet

James Paisible
(c.1650–1721)
arr. Bergmann

The cheerful soldier

Hermann Berens
(1826–1880)
arr. Adams

Waltz variations

Benjamin Britten
(1913–1976)
arr. Bergmann

Var. II

Babiole

Jean-Jacques Naudot
(c.1690–1762)
arr. Bergmann

Gavotte

George Frideric Handel
(1685–1759)

Polka

Czech traditional
arr. Bergmann

Andante

from *Partita* No. 1

Georg Philipp Telemann
(1681–1767)
arr. Bergmann

Slater's fancy

English Country Dance
(1719)
arr. Bergmann

Pastourelle

Georg Philipp Telemann
(1681–1767)
arr. Bergmann

At sunset

Paolo Conte
(1890–1966)
arr. Adams

Sunny spells

Paul Harris

Gavotte

Johann Christoph Pepusch
(1667–1752)
arr. Bergmann

Partie: I Pastorale

Joseph Haydn
(1732–1809)
arr. Bergmann

Partie: III Finale

Joseph Haydn
(1732–1809)
arr. Bergmann

Hungarian melody
from *Songs and dances* Op. 33, No. 11

Adolf Jensen
(1837–1879)
arr. Adams

Moody Judy

Ned Bennett

Pastourelle

Georg Philipp Telemann
(1681–1767)
arr. Bergmann

At sunset

Paolo Conte
(1890–1966)
arr. Adams

12

Sunny spells

Paul Harris

© 2004 by Faber Music Ltd.

Gavotte

Johann Christoph Pepusch
(1667–1752)
arr. Bergmann

© 1980 by Faber Music Ltd.

Partie: I Pastorale

Joseph Haydn
(1732–1809)
arr. Bergmann

Partie: III Finale

Joseph Haydn
(1732–1809)
arr. Bergmann

Coffee bean carnival!

Sarah Watts

Hungarian melody
from *Songs and dances* Op. 33, No. 11

Adolf Jensen
(1837–1879)
arr. Adams

Moody Judy

Ned Bennett

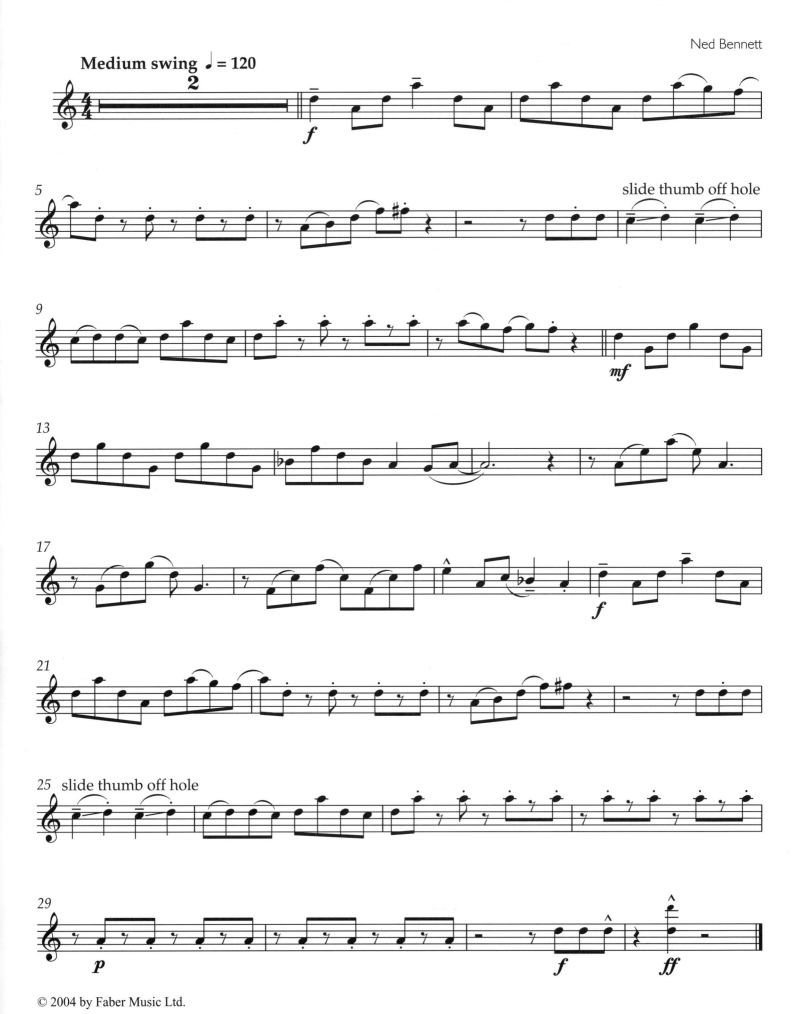

FIRST REPERTOIRE FOR
DESCANT RECORDER

Descant recorder part

edited and selected by
ausgewählt und herausgegeben von
choisi et édité par

Sally Adams

FABER *ff* MUSIC

CONTENTS

Off to somewhere

Sarah Watts

© 2004 by Faber Music Ltd.

Les bouffons

from *Orchésographie* (1589)

Traditional,
arr. Bergmann

© 1980 by Faber Music Ltd.

4

Pony trot

Walter Bergmann

Hot coffee at the Silver Spoon Corral

Sally Adams

Austrian ländler

Walter Bergmann

Waltzing echidna

An echidna is an Australian animal with spikes, somewhat like a hedgehog.

Elissa Milne

Thumbs up!

Doris da Costa

Theme

from Theme and variations for flute and strings

Saverio Mercadante
(1795–1870)
arr. Adams

Moderato

Monty

(The mystery cat)

Pam Wedgwood

Jauntily   poco rit.   a tempo

Musette

Esprit Philippe Chèdeville
(1696–1762)
arr. Bergmann

Moderato

p legato

Fine   **D.C. al Fine**

Minuet

James Paisible
(c.1650–1721)
arr. Bergmann

Tempo di menuetto

© 1980 by Faber Music Ltd.

The cheerful soldier

Hermann Berens
(1826–1880)
arr. Adams

Allegro moderato

© 2004 by Faber Music Ltd.

Waltz variations

Benjamin Britten
(1913–1976)
arr. Bergmann

Babiole

Jean-Jacques Naudot
(c.1690–1762)
arr. Bergmann

Gavotte

George Frideric Handel
(1685–1759)

Jumping Jacks

Doris da Costa

Polka

Czech traditional
arr. Bergmann

'Andante' from *Partita* No. 1

Georg Philipp Telemann
(1681–1767)
arr. Bergmann

Slater's fancy

English Country Dance
(1719)
arr. Bergmann

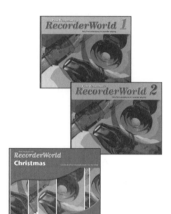